KILLER OF HER HUSBAND'S SECRETARY

The 1935 Love Triangle Ire
of Etta Reisman

(A Historical True Crime Short)

R. BARRI FLOWERS

KILLER OF HER HUSBAND'S SECRETARY
The 1935 Love Triangle Ire of Etta Reisman
(A Historical True Crime Short)

ISBN: 1722777605
ISBN-13: 978-1722777609

TRUE CRIME TITLES BY R. BARRI FLOWERS

Dead at the Saddleworth Moor
Killers of the Lonely Hearts
Mass Murder in the Sky
Missing or Murdered
Murder at the Pencil Factory
Murder During the Chicago World's Fair
Murder of a Star Quarterback
Murder of the Banker's Daughter
Murder of the Doctor's Wife
Murder of the Horse Trainer's Rival
Murder of the U.S. Attorney
Murdered by the King of Western Swing
Murderess on the Loose
Murders in the United States
Serial Killer Couples
The Amityville Massacre
The Dreadful Acts of Jack the Ripper
The Gold Special Train Robbery
The Pickaxe Killers
The Sex Slave Murders (1, 2, & 3)

MYSTERY & THRILLER FICTION TITLES BY R. BARRI FLOWERS

Before He Kills Again: A Veronica Vasquez Thriller
Dark Streets of Whitechapel: A Jack the Ripper Mystery
Dead in Pukalani: An Eddie Naku Maui Mystery
Dead in Kihei: An Eddie Naku Maui Mystery
Deadly Defense: A Grace Gaynor Christian Mystery
Justice Served: A Barkley & Parker Mystery
Murder in Maui: A Leila Kahana Mystery
Murder on Kaanapali Beach: A Leila Kahana Mystery
Murder of the Hula Dancers: A Leila Kahana Mystery
Persuasive Evidence: A Jordan La Fontaine Legal Thriller
State's Evidence: A Beverly Mendoza Legal Thriller

PRAISE FOR TRUE CRIME BOOKS BY R. BARRI FLOWERS

"Selected as one of Suspense Magazine's Best books." —John Raab, CEO/Publisher on *The Sex Slave Murders*

"A gripping account of the murders committed by husband-and-wife serial killers Gerald and Charlene Gallego." — Gary C. King, true crime author on *The Sex Slave Murders*

"Vivid case studies of murder to complement this well researched criminology text." — Scott Bonn, Ph.D., criminology professor on *The Dynamics of Murder*

"A model of exposition not to be missed by anyone interested in the annals of American criminal behavior." —Jim Ingraham, Ph.D., professor emeritus of American Studies at Bryant University on *The Pickaxe Killers*

"R. Barri Flowers always relates an engrossing story." —Robert Scott, true crime author on *The Sex Slave Murders*

"Striking, well-written tales sparkle in this ocean of murder." — Diane Fanning, true crime author on *Masters of True Crime*

"Would appeal to public library true-crime buffs." — Booklist on *Murders in the United States*

"Exhaustively researched, each storyteller brings their own unique prose to these pages, creating what will soon become a true crime classic." — Kevin M. Sullivan, true crime author on *Masters of True Crime*

"This book should be a mandatory purchase and read for any true-crime buff." — Steven A. Egger, Ph.D., associate professor on *Masters of True Crime*

"Incredible cases, psychopathic killers, unwitting victims, along with the very best writers, make for an exciting, no-holds-barred, soon-to-be true-crime classic." — Dan Zupansky, host of True Murder on *Masters of True Crime*

"An indispensable sourcebook for anyone interested in American homicide, from law-enforcement professionals to armchair criminologists." — Harold Schechter, true crime historian on *The Dynamics of Murder*

* * *

In memory of Virginia Seigh and other tragic victims of historical and present-day love triangle fatalities and unexpectedly shortened lives.

* * *

CONTENTS

KILLER OF HER HUSBAND'S SECRETARY
The 1935 Love Triangle Ire of Etta Reisman

On the morning of Wednesday, August 14, 1935, Virginia Seigh, an attractive twenty-three-year-old secretary, was shot and killed as she stood in the driveway of a home in Queens, New York. Her murderer was Mrs. Etta Reisman, the thirty-five-year-old wife of Arthur Reisman, a forty-two-year-old well-to-do owner of a beauty salon chain.[1] The previous day, Reisman had confessed to his wife that he had fallen in love with Miss Seigh—his secretary, who had resided with the Reismans for seven years—and wanted a separation. This did not set well with Etta, who felt totally betrayed by her husband and their house guest, causing her to snap and go on a shooting frenzy. Along with Reisman himself, also witnessing the shocking homicide was his daughter from an earlier marriage, Annette Reisman. The twenty-three-year-old was injured when she attempted to take the gun from the unhinged shooter. Etta Reisman was arrested and charged with murder in this classic case of a love triangle that ended tragically for all parties concerned. The embittered wife turned vengeful killer was convicted of the crime of violence, resulting in a stunning and controversial action the judge set in motion. The heartbreaking tale of Etta Reisman has endured through the decades as, sadly, many others have followed the same path of jealous rage as an often impulsive and deadly response to being wronged and paying an even greater price themselves in the final analysis.

* * *

The year of 1935 brought about some memorable achievements in American society. On Friday, January 11th, pioneer aviator Amelia Earhart flew solo from Honolulu, Hawaii, to Oakland, California, becoming the first pilot to do so.[2]

On Thursday, May 30, 1935, George Herman Ruth Jr., better known as Babe Ruth, baseball great and future Hall of Famer, played his final game in the majors for the Boston Braves against the Philadelphia Phillies in Philadelphia, Pennsylvania.[3] On Thursday, June 13th, James Walter Braddock won the world heavyweight championship by defeating Max Baer at New York City's Madison Square Garden Bowl.

On Wednesday, August 14th, the Social Security Act of 1935 was signed into law by President Franklin D. Roosevelt, and on Saturday, November 30th, the British film, "Scrooge," "the first all-talking film version of Charles Dickens' classic, *A Christmas Carol*, open[ed] in the U.S. after its British release."[4]

That year was also marked by a number of notable crime-related stories in this country. On Thursday, January 3, 1935, in what was called the "Trial of the Century," Bruno Richard Hauptmann went on trial in Flemington, New Jersey, for the kidnapping and murder of twenty-month-old Charles Lindbergh Jr., son of famed aviator Charles Lindbergh.[5] Hauptmann was convicted and executed in April of the following year.

On Wednesday, January 16, 1935, the infamous Depression-era Barker Gang and its family matriarch Kate Barker, often referred to as Ma Barker, were gunned down by the FBI in the course of a last stand shootout at a house in Ocklawaha, Florida.[6]

On Sunday, September 8th, Huey Pierce Long Jr., U.S. Senator and former governor of Louisiana, was assassinated in Baton Rouge at the Louisiana State Capitol by physician Carl Austin Weiss Sr., who was also shot and killed that same day by the politician's bodyguards.[7]

On Monday, December 9th, American investigative journalist and newspaper editor Walter William Liggett was murdered in a gangland drive-by shooting in Minneapolis, Minnesota, with the shooter using a Thompson submachine gun.[8] Liggett wrote exposes on organized crime in the city. Mobster Isadore Blumenfeld was acquitted of the murder, in spite of witnesses and solid evidence to the contrary. No other person would ever be charged with the crime.

In the midst of these murder cases of 1935, on Wednesday, August 14th, an attractive secretary, Virginia Seigh, would be shot to death in the wee hours of the morning in the New York City Borough of Queens by a vindictive wife, Etta Reisman.

* * *

Queens originated in 1683 in being amongst the twelve counties that made up the Province of New York. "Coterminous with Queens

County since 1899, the borough of Queens...is the easternmost and largest in area of the five boroughs of New York City [and] is geographically adjacent to the borough of Brooklyn at the southwestern end of Long Island, and to Nassau County farther east on Long Island."[9] Additionally, "Queens shares water borders with the boroughs of Manhattan and the Bronx."[10]

Between 1920 and 1930, the population of Queens grew by more than 130 percent, to over a million residents. With the Great Depression, the rate of growth slowed by 1940, but still grew by more than 20 percent from 1930. Within the decade was a boom in construction in Queens. This included "the Triborough Bridge in 1936 and the Bronx-Whitestone [Bridge] in 1939...the Interboro Parkway in 1935...the Grand Central Parkway in 1936 and...LaGuardia Airport, [opening in northern Queens] in 1939."[11] Also that year, Queens hosted the 1939 New York World's Fair, with the site morphing at the fair's close into Flushing Meadows Park.[12]

In the summer of 1935, one of the best neighborhoods in Queens was called Beechhurst. It has been said that:

> During the Silent Movie era, it was a favorite vacation area for the rich and famous. Estates lined the waterfront, including those of industrialist Harvey Firestone and entertainment impresario Arthur Hammerstein.... The Beechhurst Towers hotel...was a favorite of actress Mary Pickford and was frequented by many Broadway and early movie stars, including the Marx Brothers and W. C. Fields.[13]

With its nice homes and well-manicured lawns, Beechhurst was located in the northeastern part of the borough of Queens as a desirable place to call home.

The early morning of Wednesday, August 14th of that year could have been like any other morning for local residents, whether asleep, still awake, or otherwise. But it turned out to be anything but normal.

This was especially true for the residents of 14-37 Utopia Parkway. Living in the posh brick house that was two and a half stories tall with a backyard swimming pool, were forty-two-year-old Arthur Reisman, the balding, successful owner of six beauty parlors; his wife of twelve years, Etta Reisman, age thirty-five; their nine-year-old son, Elias; Reisman's twenty- three-year-old daughter, Annette Reisman, whom he had fathered with his first wife who was now deceased; and his live-in secretary, twenty-three-year-old Virginia Seigh.

Unfortunately, Reisman found himself smitten with his much younger and striking blonde secretary, and apparently vice versa. A day earlier, he had informed his stunned wife that he was in love with Virginia and offered Etta the sum of $30 a week, if she would only consent to a separation.

While she had evidently begrudgingly accepted the offer, by the next day, Etta had a change of heart. More likely, the idea of giving up her husband to his attractive secretary who had lived in their house for seven years and betrayed her trust in the worst way, was never seriously considered by Etta.

Instead, she was much more intent on stopping Reisman from moving on with his new life at her expense. Or at least preventing Virginia from ever taking away what was hers.

Armed with a gun, Etta confronted the younger woman outside the house. Fearing for her life, Virginia cowered in the driveway before Etta, without much ado, opened fire, shooting her husband's lover to death. Looking on in disbelief was Etta's stepdaughter, Annette. She suffered an injury to her hand when making a valiant effort to take the weapon out of Etta's hands.

As the murder took place, Arthur Reisman sat in his vehicle close by, apparently not believing that things could escalate to this tragic turn of events until it was too late. A little earlier, he had supposedly told his wife with a note of finality about the young woman residing with them "first as a matter of business convenience" before things developed well beyond that: "I love Virginia and Virginia loves me!"[14]

Now, in seeing his beloved lying on the lawn, a single bullet having gone into her heart, Reisman "threw his arms around the slain girl" and screamed at Etta in disbelief: "You don't know what you've done, you've killed my dearest in cold blood—"[15]

Indeed, it was a sad ending for Virginia Seigh, who would never live to have a life with Arthur Reisman and all that it may have entailed.

In the meantime, Etta Reisman was hysterical while still holding the revolver belonging to her husband. But, apparently, she was satisfied with killing his paramour secretary and did not seek to turn the weapon on him or herself.

She would soon be taken into custody for murdering Miss Seigh, the rival for her husband's affections.

* * *

That same morning, a tearful Etta Reisman—wearing a blue gingham dress, bare-legged and hatless, along with beach sandals—was arraigned in the Flushing Court before Magistrate Giorgio. She was ordered held without bail.

Queens County District Attorney Charles P. Sullivan sought further investigation of the crime in conferring with Assistant District Attorney William H. Barr, while contemplating whether to charge the suspect with murder in the first degree or manslaughter and postponing taking the case to a grand jury.

Meanwhile, Etta's defense attorney, Sydney Rosenthal, who hoped to have an adjournment of the case till after Labor Day, indicated his defense of the accused would be based upon "a plea of emotional insanity."[16]

In spite of witnessing the shooting death of his lover, Arthur Reisman threw his support behind his spouse, insisting: "Etta is my wife and I'm going to defend her with every dollar I've got or can raise. Etta's mind was poisoned.... She is a good woman...."[17]

As it was, Reisman faced a tall order in defending what appeared to be the indefensible, apart from a love triangle as justification for murder. According to Etta Reisman in her chilling confession to the crime, she confronted Virginia, who stood frightened in the driveway wearing "pink satin pajamas," and asked her bluntly: "Virginia, tell me the truth. Do you love my husband and does he love you...?"[18] When she uttered, "Yes," to the question, Etta reacted in the following manner, as laid out by the *New York Times* in its August 15, 1935, story:

> She lifted the pistol with both hands and fired one shot at Miss Seigh, who was only about three feet away from her. Miss Seigh staggered along the driveway...and collapsed on the lawn. Annette went after Mrs. Reisman, who was retreating...and tried to wrest the pistol from her. In the struggle, the weapon went off, inflicting a slight wound on [Annette's] little finger of her left hand. Mrs. Reisman said she fired the remaining cartridges into the [garage] door...[and] went into the house [where she] telephoned...the doctor and the police.[19]

In an autopsy on Virginia Seigh, conducted by Assistant Medical Examiner Dr. Richard Grimes, it was found that "a bullet had pierced her heart and right lung," killing her.[20] The body was transported to the Brooklyn home of Clarence P. Seigh, the victim's father, on East Twenty-Second Street.

On Saturday, August 17, 1935, Virginia Seigh, whom her stepmother lamented was "pure as a lily," was laid to rest in Braddock, Pennsylvania, a town near Pittsburgh that the Seigh family resided in previously.[21]

Virginia was born and raised in North Braddock, before the family relocated to Brooklyn in 1923 when her father received a transfer in his job for Westinghouse Company as a turbine engineer. At the Second Ward School she went to, classmates remembered her as a "pretty brunette [and] popular," who had returned to Braddock to visit an aunt in the summer of 1934.[22] Accompanying her on the trip was Annette Reisman, with whom she had become good friends.

Sadly, Virginia's mother had died in 1920. Virginia was buried next to her at Monongahela Cemetery—and it was a life that had ended much too soon.

In the meantime, her killer, an emotionally broken Etta Reisman, was being held at the

Jefferson Market Prison for women. There, in spite of the rather dire situation she had put herself in, the murder suspect was quoted as saying coldly: "I'm glad I did it. I couldn't let her steal my husband."[23]

And with the ultimate payback, Etta's own date with destiny had yet to play out.

* * *

On Monday, August 19, 1935, District Attorney Sullivan announced "that he would seek a first-degree murder indictment against Mrs. Etta Reisman," for the killing of "her husband's secretary, Virginia Seigh, on the lawn of the Reisman home at 14-37 Utopia Parkway [in] Queens."[24] On Friday, September 6th, the "grand jury [was] sworn in [and] the case against Mrs. Reisman would be presented before that body on the same day..."[25]

In an interesting twist that presented itself in Flushing Court that day with Magistrate Giorgio on the bench, it was revealed that the police were called to the Reisman's home at 12:30 a.m. on August 14th, shortly before the deadly encounter, by Annette, out of concern that her father was inebriated and argumentative. She and Etta were allegedly told to "go to the Bayside Precinct in the morning, if they wanted to make a complaint."[26]

According to defense counsel Rosenthal, Etta Reisman warned the police that "there was a revolver in the house...[and] asked the police to take the revolver with them."[27] As such, it was his intent to make this an issue in the case by placing part of the onus for the tragedy on the authorities, while also using a temporary insanity defense in arguing against premeditation in the killing of Miss Seigh.

While Assistant District Attorney Barr acknowledged that Etta told the police that her husband had a gun, he also zeroed in on the murder suspect's confession, in which she admitted to gazing out the living room window where Virginia and Annette stood on the lawn seeking to calm down Reisman, who was sitting in his vehicle.

According to Etta, she could hear the three talking, with her husband saying: "Virginia, let us tell her everything," followed by Virginia admitting to Annette: "Yes, I love your father and your father loves me."[28]

This stark admission was apparently more than Etta Reisman could bear, as she snapped in anger and "immediately went upstairs to the bedroom, took the revolver, and descending by a side stair to the lawn, confronted the secretary."[29] Shortly thereafter, Virginia Seigh was shot dead before Annette and Reisman's very eyes.

On Thursday, September 19th, Etta Reisman was indicted in Queens County Court before Judge Charles S. Colden by the grand jury for second-degree murder in the shooting death of Virginia Seigh at around two a.m. on August 14th.[30]

During her arraignment, Etta pleaded not guilty through her attorney, Sydney Rosenthal, who conversed with the Chief Assistant District Attorney James J. Conroy about the particulars of the trial.

The tentative date to commence the trial was set by Judge Colden for Monday, October 14, 1935. In the meantime, Etta Reisman was released from custody on $15,000 bail.[31]

* * *

On Monday, December 16, 1935, thirty-five-year-old Etta Reisman went on trial in Queens County Court, with Judge Charles Colden on the bench, for the murder of twenty-three-year-old Virginia Seigh. The jury was composed of eleven married men and one single male to decide the fate of the accused.

On behalf of the State, Assistant District Attorney Irwin J. Shapiro laid out the prosecution's case, in which it planned to "prove that [the defendant's] jealousy toward her husband's youthful secretary was the motive which...impelled Mrs. Reisman to shoot the rival for her husband's affections."[32] In this regard, the State intended to "show that [the defendant] first obtained her husband's revolver, loaded it, went out onto the lawn, where her husband['s]...daughter, [Annette Reisman] and Miss Seigh [were] standing, and after asking one question [to the victim], fired pointblank at Miss Seigh."[33]

In his opening statement, Etta Reisman's defense counsel Rosenthal argued that, in fact, it was the defendant's intention to commit suicide on that fateful morning, but in the attempt to grab hold of the firearm and the ensuing fracas by Arthur Reisman and her stepdaughter, Annette, to that effect, the gun went off accidentally and fatally, hitting Virginia Seigh.

According to Rosenthal, shortly before the deadly encounter:

> On [that] morning Mrs. Reisman heard what her husband had always protested was untrue: the statement of the love of this man and girl for each other. [The defendant] obtained the gun and walked out on the lawn where her husband, his daughter, and his sweetheart were

> standing.... Exclaiming that she wished to live no longer, Mrs. Reisman pointed the gun at her own head. Annette grasped the gun by the barrel. As Mrs. Reisman pulled one way and Annette another, the gun went off. No one knew at the time that Virginia was shot.[34]

The prosecution called a number of law enforcement witnesses to the stand to support its case against the defendant. Amongst these were Detective Sergeant Henry Butts, the ballistics bureau chief of the police department. He testified that the murder weapon was "held from four to six inches away from the point where the bullet entered Miss Seigh's body."[35]

Also testifying were Bayside Precinct patrolmen Henry G. Wehman and Francis J. Mooney, who contended that the defendant was in the living room when they arrived, and apparently could not seem to remember what she did with the murder weapon. It was eventually located in "a bedroom concealed beneath a pillow...wrapped in a towel."[36]

* * *

On Wednesday, December 18th, called as a defense witness was Dr. Clarence J. Cehen, the Reismans' family physician, "who had treated [Etta] for nervous hysteria [and whose testimony characterized] the emotions that [boiled] within the breast of the housewife, and the strife that raged within the prim suburban bungalow, overlooking the placid water of Long Island Sound."[37]

Also testifying for the defense were twelve women. Referred to as the "unofficial jury," they came to Etta's aide as character witnesses, all of whom were "Queens housewives whose station in life [were] similar to the defendant's."[38] According to the women, Etta Reisman was very much like them, "respected [and] regarded as a lady," with her reputation described as "'"excellent,' 'very good,' 'above reproach,' and 'just perfect.'"[39]

According to one observer, as the defendant listened to the heartfelt testimony, "the ceaseless, monotonous tears of Mrs. Reisman, huddled beside an erect police matron, gave evidence of remorse.... So did the strained face of bald-headed Arthur Reisman, loved by the woman, and the soft sobs of his daughter, Annette, friend of the dead girl."[40]

In the afternoon, Etta Reisman was called to the stand by her lawyer, Rosenthal, to testify in her own defense. She testified she had long suspected that her husband and Virginia were having an affair or "since a year after [Miss]

Seigh came to live [with them] as a girlhood companion of her stepdaughter, Annette."[41]

Etta claimed that on the day of the deadly encounter, she looked out the window and, while her husband held Virginia in his comforting arms, listened irately as he told the young woman: "Let's make a clean breast of it; let's tell Annette everything; you understand, I can't live without you—"[42] The defendant then described how, in her distraught state, she "went to the holster where the pistol hung, replaced the shells, and walked out onto the driveway."[43]

Etta testified that she put the gun up to her head and attempted to take her own life, but was interrupted from pulling the trigger by Annette, who grabbed her arm and wrestled her for the weapon, when it went off, striking Virginia accidentally. According to the defendant, shortly thereafter, Arthur screeched at her: "You've killed the only girl in the world I've ever loved—"[44]

Under cross-examination, Etta maintained her story of a suicide gone awry and an accidental shooting "almost word for word, [while] den[ying] vigorously that it had been rehearsed," as was believed by the prosecution.[45]

The case went to the jury, with the defendant's fate hanging in the balance.

* * *

On Friday, December 20, 1935, the jury found thirty-five-year-old Etta Reisman guilty of manslaughter in the first degree for killing her husband's secretary, Virginia Seigh, the twenty-three-year-old competition for Arthur Reisman's affections and loyalty. Though the jury recommended that the guilty woman be given clemency, she faced anywhere from ten to twenty years behind bars.[46]

Having been led into court by matron Mae Winkler, the convicted killer "looked haggard, but took the verdict calmly."[47] The same was not true for two others directly involved in the fatal event. Upon hearing the verdict, Annette Reisman "burst into tears, while [Etta's] husband, Arthur," who along with Miss Seigh had "openly confessed their love" for each other, leading to the tragedy, "put his right hand to his lips as though to stifle an outcry...[and] wandered about the courtroom as if in a daze."[48]

Pending her sentencing, Etta remained in custody at the Manhattan Women's House of Detention facility. That afternoon, she met with John Butler, the chief probation officer, at the Queens County Court, which was standard practice for inmates with a felony conviction in assisting the judge in the decision-making process for sentencing.

* * *

Queens County Court Judge Charles Colden was under pressure from a number of prominent and sympathetic women who lived in the prosperous Beechhurst and Whitestone neighborhood of Queens to grant Etta Reisman clemency, circulating petitions to that effect.[49]

In speaking for the Beechhurst Women's Club of Queens, its leader, Mrs. George Bornkessel, defended their position: "I knew Mrs. Reisman as a member of the women's club. I found her to be sweet, unassuming and always active in the best things the club promoted. We feel she should be given the extreme limit of leniency in the matter of sentence."[50] This strong support of Etta Reisman by her peers was in addition to the all-male jury recommending mercy for the convicted killer in a crime of passion.

On Monday, December 23, 1935, Judge Colden sentenced Etta to six to twelve years of incarceration in the Bedford Hills Correctional Facility for Women, located in Westchester County, New York, for taking the life of Virginia Seigh.[51] However, in relenting to the betrayed wife's supporters, believing she had been wronged and deserved leniency, the judge suspended the sentence.

More specifically, Judge Colden proclaimed, as the defendant stood before him as ordered: "It is the sentence of this court, Etta Reisman, that you be confined in prison for no less than six years and no more than twelve years." Following a thoughtful pause, he then uttered shockingly to most in the courtroom: "Execution of sentence is stayed..."[52]

Due to the legal ambiguity of his words, Etta, along with some other observers in the dramatic moment, apparently mistook this as meaning she was headed to prison. While being led to an antechamber by a couple of court attaches, she faltered and sobbed uncontrollably. Upon reaching the anteroom, Etta passed out, still sure that she would not be going home anytime soon.

When she regained consciousness twenty minutes later, Etta learned to her total disbelief that the judge had, in fact, set her free to be with her now ten-year-old son, Elias, and presumably her husband, Arthur Reisman, and stepdaughter, Annette, neither of whom had been in attendance in the courtroom to hear the ruling in spite of their steady presence during the entire trial. Though neither Reisman nor Annette, as eyewitnesses to the shooting death of Virginia, had been called to testify by the State, both had likely anticipated the worst for the convicted wife and mother.

The same was true for Virginia Seigh's father and stepmother, Mr. and Mrs. Clarence Seigh, who were there for the sentencing and left in disbelief that there would be no justice for their daughter and her premature death.

As his explanation for rendering the suspension of a prison term, Judge Colden calmly stated:

> The purpose of a sentence is to punish and rehabilitate. But Etta Reisman has been punished for [seven] years, ever since Virginia Seigh appeared in her household. [Mrs. Reisman] has a splendid character and is a good mother and needs no rehabilitation. And she has had her punishment. Therefore, I accept the recommendation of the jury and exercise clemency.[53]

With the stay, while Etta escaped prison time, she was neither on probation nor parole, but rather "the sentence [would] remain in force throughout her lifetime and become operative if she [were] again convicted of a crime."[54]

In spite of the satisfaction of many with the controversial ruling by the judge, not everyone applauded this or felt it was legally sound. According to the Court of General Sessions Judge James G. Wallace and a number of other judges, suspending the sentence was illegal, bolstering their argument with "Section 2188 of the Penal Code," which read in part: "...neither sentence, nor the execution thereof, shall be suspended...if the person is convicted of a felony committed while armed with a weapon as provided in Section 1944...."[55]

This notwithstanding, Judge Colden did not budge from the suspended sentence, arguing that "he had never known a case which had caused him more concern."[56]

Furthermore, he argued that he did have legal standing for his decision: "It is my opinion that the legislature intended the provision of the homicide law to be all-inclusive and my sentence was based strictly on the law as I found it. I did not suspend the sentence. I gave the sentence but stayed the execution."[57]

In backing up the stay, Assistant District Attorney Harry I. Huber pointed out the jury's plea for mercy along with "the splendid reputation of the defendant," in the District Attorney's office's decision not to fight the clemency given to Etta Reisman.[58]

* * *

Following her shocking release from custody, a contented Etta indicated to the *New York Times* that she planned to take her son, Elias, to Atlantic City for the Christmas holiday and eventually hoped to "enter the beauty parlor business with the financial backing of her brothers."[59] With respect to getting back together with her husband, Arthur Reisman—whom she was willing to kill another woman to keep as her own—Etta had changed her tune, uttering impassively: "I've taken all the punishment I'm going to take. I think it best that he go his way and I go mine."[60]

On Friday, March 13, 1936, Clarence Seigh, father of slain secretary Virginia Seigh, made a public appeal to pressure the criminal justice system into resentencing Etta Reisman, who got off scot-free in spite of her conviction for manslaughter. Seigh had previously pleaded his case to the Queens County District Attorney Charles Sullivan, Governor Herbert H. Lehman, and Speaker of the New York State Assembly Irving McNeil Ives, all to no avail, as they argued that the law as it stood and Colden's discretionary power had "tied their hands," in effect.[61]

Seigh insisted that retribution was not his objective in this matter: "I am not [driven] by motives of vengeance, but rather by the resolve to do everything in my power to see that such a miscarriage of justice may not occur again in the State of New York."[62]

On Thursday, October 27, 1938, New York State Supreme Court Justice George H. Furman rejected a further attempt to reverse the ruling in favor of convicted killer Etta Reisman by denying "an application for a writ of mandamus which would compel County Judge Charles Colden to execute a sentence he suspended in the case of Mrs. Etta Reisman three years ago."[63] In the ruling, Furman held that with regard to the writ initiated by District Attorney Sullivan, who now argued that the "suspension of sentence was illegal," and the "action sought had been outlawed by the legislature and that the statute of limitations concerning a mandamus had expired."[64]

With her freedom assured, Etta Reisman, who had relocated to a home in Sullivan County, New York, in a hamlet called Livingston Manor, continued to live her life apparently apart from Arthur Reisman, the man she once loved with all her heart, and well removed from the jealous rage killing of former rival, Virginia Seigh.

As for Miss Seigh, she would be remembered as the tragic victim of young love and a crime of passion, for which her life and times would be forever shattered.

# # #

SERIAL KILLER COUPLES

Bonded by Sexual Depravity, Abduction, and Murder

(bonus chapter from the bestselling true crime anthology)

Paul Bernardo and Karla Homolka

Paul Bernardo and Karla Homolka were Canadian sex-motivated serial killers whose brutal crimes shocked the nation. They kidnapped, sexually assaulted, tortured, and murdered at least three teenage girls in the early 1990s, including Homolka's own sister. The killer couple was also suspected of perpetrating a number of other violent attacks on women.

Bernardo's reign of terror began with sexual attacks in and around Scarborough, a municipality within Toronto, Ontario. Dubbed by the press as the "Scarborough Rapist," he perpetrated numerous rapes, escalating into murder with the assistance of his partner in crime, Karla Homolka. A storybook romance between Bernardo and Homolka turned into a nightmare of domestic and sexual violence, along with cold-blooded murder that ensured the disturbing pair a place in the annals of infamous serial killer couples.

* * *

Paul Kenneth Bernardo was born August 27, 1964, in Toronto, Canada, a product of an affair between his married mother and a previous boyfriend. Her husband, Kenneth Bernardo, who owned a thriving marble and tile business, was listed on Bernardo's birth certificate as his biological father, in spite of apparently knowing otherwise.

Kenneth Bernardo was the perpetrator of domestic violence against his wife and child abuse toward his children, including sexually molesting his own daughter. He was charged with child molestation for fondling a girl. All this sent Bernardo's mother into depression. By outward appearances, Paul Bernardo seemed less impacted by the abuse during childhood, described as "always happy [and] smiled a lot.... He was the perfect child they all wanted: polite, well mannered, doing well in school, so sweet in his Boy Scout uniform."[1]

However, upon learning at age sixteen that Kenneth Bernardo was not his real father, Bernardo reportedly called his mother a "whore."

Upon graduating from Sir Wilfrid Laurier Collegiate Institute, Bernardo found work with Amway, embracing their sales techniques. He and friends applied these techniques on women in bars and apparently succeeded, often seducing them. Once he started college at the University of Toronto Scarborough, Bernardo had already "developed dark sexual fantasies, enjoyed humiliating women in public and beating up the women he dated."[2]

While in college, Bernardo also engaged in other criminal activity for profit, such as smuggling cigarettes with friends across the Canadian-U.S. border, and would later seek other means of making money illegally.

After graduating, Bernardo found employment at Price Waterhouse as a junior accountant. His sexual dark side remained active, turning to sexual assaults. Between May and July of 1987, he raped at least three young women in the Scarborough area, with his method of operation often being to stalk victims at night once they got off buses. He became known as the "Scarborough Rapist."

In October 1987, twenty-three-year-old Bernardo first laid eyes on seventeen-year-old, blonde, attractive Karla Homolka. By most accounts, there was an instant mutual attraction. This would set the stage for their future perverse homicidal relationship.

* * *

Born on May 4, 1970, in Port Credit, Ontario, Canada, Karla Leanne Homolka was the oldest of three daughters. The family resided in St. Catharines, Ontario, thirty-two miles south of Toronto across Lake Ontario.

Homolka attended Sir Winston Churchill Secondary School, while doing part-time work at a pet shop. After graduating in 1988, she went to work as a veterinary assistant at Thorold Veterinary Clinic; followed by similar type work at the Martindale Animal Clinic.

On October 17, 1987, Karla Homolka and Paul Bernardo met at a restaurant in Scarborough while both were attending a Toronto convention. They became quickly attracted sexually. Homolka seemingly had no problem with Bernardo's sadistic sexual desires, unlike most of the previous girls he had dated.

At one point in the relationship, a curious and confident Bernardo asked Homolka what her thoughts would be if she knew he was a rapist. Apparently she gave her approval, encouraging him to continue what had started before she came into the picture—sexually assaulting women. Which, in and of itself, was a prelude to sexual murders the pair would perpetrate in unison.

* * *

Between December 1987 and May 1990, Paul Bernardo raped or attempted to rape at least twelve teenagers and young women. It was in this respect that authorities were initially on the hunt for the unknown suspect called the Scarborough Rapist. Metropolitan Toronto Police Detective Constable Steve Irwin was one of the lead detectives in the investigation.

After the rape of a fifteen-year-old girl on December 16, 1987, a warning was issued by the Toronto Police Service for women in Scarborough who traveled alone at night, particularly those who took buses.

In another instance, on May 25, 1988, a uniformed Metro Toronto Police investigator, who was on a stake out at a bus shelter, noticed a man hiding beneath a tree. The man turned out to be Paul Bernardo. Though the investigator went after him, Bernardo managed to escape.

On November 17, 1988, a special task force was formed by the Metro Toronto Police with a mission to apprehend the Scarborough Rapist.

After a nineteen-year-old woman was raped by Bernardo on May 26, 1990, the victim was able to accurately describe her assailant, enabling the authorities to create a computer composite image of the suspect. Two days later, police released the picture and it was published in local newspapers. There was also a $50,000 reward offered in hopes of identifying and capturing the serial rapist.

In July 1990, following tips that Bernardo matched the composite of the Scarborough Rapist, Detective Constable Irwin and another detective interviewed him. Samples were taken of his blood, hair, and saliva, which were compared with 230 samples taken from additional suspects. Though Bernardo and four other suspects' samples fell within the blood group of the rapist, a case was not pursued against Paul Bernardo at that point, leaving him to continue his sexual assaults on women.

On November 20, 1990, Bernardo was interviewed again by detectives as a suspected rapist. He voluntarily supplied samples for DNA testing, and coolly handled himself as a man with nothing to hide. It was decided that "such a well-educated, well-adjusted, congenial young man could not be responsible for the vicious crimes," and Bernardo was set free the next day, having once more outsmarted his pursuers.[3]

* * *

Even while successfully dodging the police as a serial rapist in 1990, Paul Bernardo was also ingratiating himself with the family of Karla Homolka, to whom he was now engaged. Unbeknownst to the Homolkas, Bernardo had quit his accountant job at Price Waterhouse in favor of a full-time job smuggling cigarettes across the border.

That summer, he became fixated on Homolka's fifteen-year-old sister, Tammy, "peeping into her window and entering her room to masturbate while she slept."[4] Bernardo indicated to Homolka his desire to "take" Tammy's virginity, playing on Homolka's affections for him to get her cooperation. She went along with it as "an opportunity to minimize risk, take control, and keep it all in the family."[5]

On July 24, 1990, Homolka put crushed Valium, which she had stolen from her job at the Martindale Animal Clinic, in some spaghetti and served it to her sister. After Tammy passed out, Bernardo started raping her as Homolka looked on, before her sister began to awaken.

Bernardo would later reveal to Homolka that earlier in the month he had taken Tammy across the Canadian-U.S. border to buy beer, where the two "got drunk and began making out."[6]

The sexual depravity took a deadly turn on December 23, 1990. Following a Christmas party with the Homolka family, Paul Bernardo and Karla Homolka drugged Tammy Homolka with sleeping pills mixed in a cocktail of rum and eggnog. While out cold in the basement, they removed her clothing. Homolka soaked a cloth with the anesthetic agent Halothane, which she had stolen from work, and put it up to her sister's mouth and nose. Bernardo and Karla sexually assaulted the girl as her parents slept upstairs, videotaping the rape. It was supposed to be Karla's gift of her sister's "virginity to Bernardo for Christmas," because he had expressed disappointment at not being the first person Karla had sexual relations with.[7]

Tammy, her face chemically burned, would later die after choking on her own vomit. Her killers called 911, but only after they hid the evidence of the murder, put Tammy's clothes back on, and put her corpse in her bedroom in the basement.

Within a few hours, without ever having regained consciousness, Tammy Homolka was pronounced dead at St. Catharines General Hospital.

Bernardo and Homolka insisted to police that they had tried to revive Tammy. In spite of peculiar circumstances to the contrary, such as the chemical burn on the victim's face and her killers "vacuuming and washing laundry in the middle of the night," the Homolka family, authorities, and the Niagara Regional Coroner could not disprove Homolka's and Bernardo's carefully constructed story. Tammy Homolka's death was officially ruled as accidental due to choking on her vomit after consuming alcohol.[8]

Homolka and Bernardo would ultimately videotape themselves with Homolka wearing her sister's clothing while pretending she was her sister. The killer couple, who had been staying with the Homolkas, rented a bungalow on 57 Bayview Avenue in Port Dalhousie, a community in St. Catharines, while Karla's parents grieved.

* * *

On April 6, 1991, Paul Bernardo, having gotten away with rape and murder, along with his partner in crime Karla Homolka, committed his twelfth solo rape. Only, this time, instead of Scarborough, the attack occurred in St. Catharines where he and Homolka now resided.

The victim was a fourteen-year-old girl, with the rape occurring early in the morning.

Two months later, on June 7, 1991, in an attempt to please Bernardo and his sadistic sexual demands for girls, Homolka enticed seventeen-year-old "Jane Doe" (her identity is protected by law) into participating in a "girls' night out." She planned to offer the girl to Bernardo as a pre-wedding gift, with their wedding planned for the end of the month. Two years earlier, Homolka had met the girl while still employed at the animal clinic. The teenager, who considered Homolka to be a "beautiful, sophisticated role model," was only too happy to spend time with her.[9]

After lulling "Jane Doe" into a false sense of security, Homolka brought her to the house at 57 Bayview Avenue. There, she plied her with alcohol spiked with Halcion, causing the teenager to lose consciousness. Then Homolka called Bernardo and told him about this "gift" she had for him.

After undressing the virgin girl, Bernardo videotaped Homolka as she sexually assaulted the victim, then he raped and sodomized her. The next morning, the nauseous teenager vomited, believing it to be the result of drinking alcohol for the first time, unaware of the violation of her body by Homolka and Bernardo.

"Jane Doe" would visit 57 Bayview Avenue twice more, and be drugged and sexually assaulted by the couple on at least one of the occasions.

* * *

On the morning of June 15, 1991, Paul Bernardo was in the process of stealing license plates in the city of Burlington—halfway between Toronto and St. Catharines—to help in his cigarette smuggling operation when he met fourteen-year-old Leslie Mahaffy standing outside her house. She had missed curfew while attending the funeral of a friend who was killed in an automobile accident and was locked out.

Opportunistic, Bernardo struck up a conversation with the girl before luring her back to his car for a cigarette. There he abducted, blindfolded, and drove her to his house in Port Dalhousie, so he and Homolka could victimize her.

They kept Mahaffy alive for twenty-four hours, videotaping themselves as they raped, sodomized, and tortured her, before murdering the girl. Bernardo would later claim that she died from a fatal dose of Halcion administered by Homolka; whereas she contended that Mahaffy was strangled to death by Bernardo.

The following day, which was Father's Day, the serial killers moved the murdered teen's corpse from a bedroom upstairs to the basement temporarily, while playing hosts to Karla Homolka's parents and sister, Lori, who came over to the house for dinner. After they were gone, Bernardo and Homolka dismembered Mahaffy using a circular saw and encased her in cement. They dumped the cement blocks in Lake Gibson, some eleven miles south of Port Dalhousie, needing to make a number of trips to complete the grisly task.

On June 29, 1991, a father and son who were in a canoe fishing discovered one of the cement blocks near the shore of the lake. Weighing two hundred pounds, it had split open, exposing human remains. The victim was positively identified as Leslie Mahaffy with the help of her orthodontic appliance.

Her killers were on the loose and confidently believed they had gotten away with yet another brutal sexual assault and murder.

* * *

On the very day that murder victim Leslie Mahaffy was found, serial killers Paul Bernardo and Karla Homolka were married. The lavish wedding in the town of Niagara-on-the-Lake included one hundred and fifty guests, a $2,000 wedding gown for the bride, and a horse-drawn carriage ride for the newlyweds.

Only the bride and groom knew of the dark and deadly secrets they shared. And that there would likely be more victims to follow.

* * *

It was on April 16, 1992, a day before Good Friday, that Bernardo and Homolka were back on the prowl for a new sex slave as they drove through St. Catharines. Passing by Holy Cross Secondary School, a Catholic high school, the couple spotted fifteen-year-old student Kristen French walking home. Deciding she would be their next victim, they pulled the car into the nearby parking lot of Grace Lutheran Church.

Karla Homolka was the distraction, approaching the teenager while holding a map and pretending to be lost. Paul Bernardo then came up from the rear with a knife and kidnapped French, forcing her to get in the front seat of the killers' vehicle. Sitting in the back, Homolka did her part to keep the abductee in check by holding down her hair.

Bernardo and Homolka drove French to their Port Dalhousie bungalow, where she was plied with alcohol, raped, sodomized, and otherwise brutalized and tortured for three days over the Easter weekend while her kidnappers videotaped their atrocious actions. Since she was never blindfolded during her ordeal, it was clear from the start that the girl had been marked for death so she could never identify those responsible for her victimization.

The next day, Kristen French's life was ended by the serial killer couple, who then went to Easter dinner at the home of Homolka's parents. Homolka would later testify that she had watched as Bernardo strangled French to death for seven full minutes. Bernardo, in turn, claimed that Homolka "beat her with a rubber mallet because she had tried to escape and French ended up being strangled [by] a noose tied around her neck secured to a hope chest."[10]

* * *

The disappearance of Kristen French drew immediate concern from her parents and the authorities, given the teenager's daily routine of a fifteen-minute walk home from school to feed and walk her dog. The Niagara Regional Police put together a team within twenty-four hours to search the area for clues. A number of people witnessed the abduction, providing police with information to that effect. Some believed the abductors were in a Camaro. In fact, Bernardo's vehicle was a gold Nissan 240SX. A shoe belonging to French was discovered in the church parking lot, illustrating the urgency of the matter.

On April 30, 1992, the nude body of Kristen French was discovered in a ditch in Burlington, some forty-five minutes from St. Catharines and not far from the graveyard where fellow victim of the killer pair, Leslie Mahaffy, was laid to rest. French's hair had been removed and her body washed. While it was initially believed that the hair had been taken by the killers as a trophy, Homolka would insist during testimony that it had been cut merely to make identification of the victim difficult.

Nevertheless, at the moment, the killers of Kristen French and at least two other young women remained at large.

* * *

With Bernardo and Homolka having both been questioned a number of times by police regarding the Scarborough Rapist, the questionable death of Tammy Homolka, and the alleged stalking of others by Bernardo, the serial rapist-killers were undoubtedly feeling confident in their ability to evade the law. This held up on May 12, 1992, when a Niagara Regional Police sergeant and a constable interviewed Bernardo in connection with Kristen French's murder. The two quickly came to the conclusion that they were likely off base with him as a suspect, in spite of Bernardo coming clean about having been interviewed about the Scarborough rapes.

On May 15th, the Green Ribbon Task Force was set up to investigate the murder of Leslie Mahaffy and Kristen French.

In the meantime, Bernardo and Homolka, perhaps hoping to separate themselves from their murderous past and the police investigation ensuing, applied to change their last name legally to Teale—the name of a serial killer in *Criminal Law*, a 1988 movie.

By December 1992, the Centre of Forensic Sciences started testing DNA samples Bernardo had given three years before.

On December 27th, in a fit of rage, Bernardo used a flashlight to beat his wife, Karla, on the face, head, and limbs. On January 4, 1993, a still badly bruised Homolka went back to work after telling everyone she had been injured in a car accident.

Homolka's concerned parents forced her to go to St. Catharines General Hospital. Her injuries were treated and she told the Niagara Regional Police she was a victim of domestic violence. Charges were filed against Paul Bernardo, who was arrested and ultimately released on his own recognizance. Afterward, Bernardo contemplated suicide, writing a note to that effect, which a friend found and intervened. A shaken and confused Karla Homolka moved in with relatives in the city of Brampton.

* * *

More than two years after he had provided a sample, Toronto police learned that Paul Bernardo's DNA was a match with that of the Scarborough Rapist. He was quickly placed under twenty-four hour surveillance.

On February 9, 1993, Karla Homolka was interviewed by investigators from the Metro Toronto Sexual Assault Squad. She sidestepped the suspicions regarding Bernardo as a serial rapist, focusing instead on being a battered wife.

That evening, Homolka admitted to her uncle and aunt that Bernardo was the Scarborough Rapist and that the two of them were responsible for the sexual assault and murder of Leslie Mahaffy and Kristen French, including recording their rapes on videotape. She did not reveal that she and Bernardo were also culpable in the death of her sister Tammy.

However, the Niagara Regional Police reopened their investigation into the death of Tammy Homolka.

On February 11th, Karla Homolka was ready to turn against her abusive husband and accomplice to rape and murder. Her Niagara Falls attorney, George Walker, wanted full immunity from St. Catharines' Crown Attorney Ray Houlahan for Homolka's cooperation in the case against Bernardo. As with her husband, Homolka was put under twenty-four hour surveillance.

Two days later, Bernardo and Homolka had their name change approved. They were now known as Paul Jason Teale and Karla Leanne Teale.

On February 14, 1993, in a meeting with Murray Segal, director of the Crown Criminal Law Office, Walker informed him about video recordings of the rapes. Segal told him that, considering the extent of Homolka's participation in the violent crimes, there was no chance of complete immunity.

Paul Bernardo was arrested on February 17, 1993, by detectives from the Metro Sexual Assault Squad and the Green Ribbon Task Force, facing a mountain of charges. Search warrants were obtained for evidence that was limited to the serial rapist case against Bernardo, given that his connection to the homicides was considered too weak. Any videotapes found were required to be viewed in the residence.

After seventy-one days of searching, which included warrants that were updated, the only videotape authorities found had a short video of Homolka engaged in oral sex on the victim known as "Jane Doe."

Nevertheless, the case was still building against Paul Bernardo.

* * *

On May 5, 1993, Homolka was offered through her lawyer a plea bargain by the government. She would receive a twelve year sentence for manslaughter in exchange for cooperation, and was given a week to agree to it or not. Declining meant she would be charged with two counts of murder in the first degree and one count of murder in the second degree, along with other charges. Homolka and her attorney agreed to the plea deal.

On May 14, 1993, the Crown and Karla Homolka plea agreement was finalized, and Homolka opened up with investigators about the grisly details of what she knew.

Homolka suggested, for one, that Bernardo may have raped up to thirty women, double the number he was suspected of sexually assaulting. Referring to him as "the happy rapist," she claimed he had bragged about perpetrating a high number of rapes.

On May 17, 1993, with Karla Homolka's cooperation and presence, police went through the serial killer couple's house in Port Dalhousie and found key DNA evidence, along with a receipt for cement purchased by Bernardo, connecting him to the murder of Leslie Mahaffy.

The following day at an arraignment, Homolka was charged with two counts of manslaughter, while the charges against Bernardo included "two counts each of kidnapping, unlawful confinement, aggravated sexual assault, and first-degree murder, as well as one count of dismemberment."[11]

On June 28, 1993, Karla Homolka went on trial for the reduced charges she faced. A publication ban imposed by the court limited what information was made available to the public, who were kept out of the courtroom. A psychiatric report on Homolka had been influential in the plea bargain the government proposed. According to the psychologist, Homolka "knew what was happening but she felt totally helpless and unable to act in her own defense or in anyone else's defense. She was in my opinion paralyzed with fear and in that state became obedient and self-serving."[12]

Given the nature of the crimes and Homolka's suspected role, the relatively light sentence did not set well with many, prompting a statement at the proceedings from Murray Segal, who sought to justify the plea bargain: "Why not a greater penalty in light of the horrendous facts? [Because,] without her, the true state of affairs might never be known. A guilty plea is the traditional hallmark of remorse. Her age, her lack of criminal record, the abuse and the influence of her husband, and her somewhat secondary role were factors. She's unlikely to re-offend."[13]

The plea bargain remained intact and Homolka got off lightly relative to the anticipated fate of her husband, Paul Bernardo.

* * *

Public backlash over the plea bargain only grew once the videotapes of young women being sexually assaulted came to light and it was clear that Homolka had been far more than a passive accomplice, but in fact was as culpable in the shocking acts of sexual brutality as Bernardo. In expressing the outrage, the Canadian press referred to the plea agreement as a "Deal with the Devil."

According to Anne McGillivray, an Associate Professor of Law at the University of Manitoba, many believed that not only had Homolka "known where the videotapes were hidden, [but] that she willfully concealed the Jane Doe incidents and, most certainly, that her claims of being under Bernardo's control—a central tenet of the plea bargain—were dubious."[14]

For their part, prosecutors insisted they would never have allowed Homolka's plea bargain had they seen the disturbing videotapes beforehand.

Though most experts agree that the damaging evidence on the videotapes would have likely resulted in Karla Homolka being tried and convicted of rape and murder, in an inquiry made on the decision of prosecutors to go with the plea bargain, it was determined that they acted in a "professional and responsible" manner and the "resolution agreement" entered into with Homolka was "unassailable" under "the Criminal Code of Canada."[15]

Judge Patrick T. Galligan had summed it up, in presenting it to the Attorney General, as "the 'lesser of two evils' to deal with an accomplice rather than to be left in a situation where a violent and dangerous offender cannot be prosecuted."[16]

* * *

In May 1995, Paul Bernardo's trial began before Judge Patrick LeSage for the sexual assaults and murders of Leslie Mahaffy and Kristen French. As with Homolka's trial, a publication ban was in effect, limiting what the

Canadian media and press could present to the public. However, the ban did not extend to broadcast and print media in the United States, allowing those living in southern Ontario easy access to reporting on the trial from Buffalo, New York.

The venue for the trial was moved from St. Catharines, where the crimes took place, to Toronto. While Bernardo admitted to raping and torturing the victims, he maintained that it was Homolka who murdered them.

Homolka testified to the contrary that Bernardo had murdered Mahaffy and French, providing details in her account. Also introduced as evidence were the controversial videotapes the two made of their victims being sexually assaulted.

Bernardo's first defense attorney, Ken Murray, had withheld these for seventeen months, planning to use them to challenge Homolka's credibility during the trial. Murray, who was replaced by John Rosen as Bernardo's attorney, would later be charged with obstruction of justice and acquitted, while also facing an appearance before the Law Society of Upper Canada for a disciplinary hearing.

On September 1, 1995, with the strong case against him, including Homolka's testimony and the incriminating videotapes, Paul

Bernardo was convicted of the aggravated sexual assaults and first-degree murders of teenagers Leslie Mahaffy and Kristen French, among other charges. He was sentenced to life in prison. Bernardo would go on to be designated as a "Dangerous Offender," subjecting him to a "longer, or indefinite, term of preventive detention in order to protect the public."[17] Though he becomes eligible to apply for parole in July 2020 after spending twenty-five years behind bars, the chances Bernardo will ever go free are considered nil at best. He is currently serving his time in the segregation unit at Millhaven Institution, a maximum-security prison, in Bath, Ontario.

* * *

In February 2000, Paul Bernardo and his attorneys appealed his conviction on the grounds of evidentiary and procedural errors by Justice Patrick LeSage. These included telling the jury Bernardo was a wife batterer, and prejudicing them regarding Karla Homolka's plea bargain and her role in the crimes, arguing that it was, in fact, Homolka who murdered Kristen French and Leslie Mahaffy. On the latter point, the Crown countered that with the graphic rape videotapes, the testimony by Homolka was not "essential to a conviction for murder."[18]

Bernardo's request for a new trial was dismissed by the Ontario Court of Appeal in March 2000. Attorneys for the families of Mahaffy and French believed the decision meant there would likely be no further appeals of the case by Bernardo.

However, the convicted murderer did appeal the conviction to the Supreme Court of Canada, which rejected it in September 2000.

Apart from the deaths of Mahaffy, French, and Tammy Homolka, along with the Scarborough rapes, Paul Bernardo has been implicated in several other violent crimes of rape and murder. These include sexually assaulting a woman in Hawaii while Bernardo and Homolka were on their honeymoon and an attack on a fifteen-year-old girl in 1987, for which he confessed in 2006, causing another man's conviction for the crime to eventually be overturned by the Court of Appeal for Ontario. Also, according to Bernardo's attorney Tony Bryant in February 2006, his client took credit for at least ten other sexual assaults during an October 2005 confession.[19]

* * *

After testifying against Paul Bernardo in 1995, Karla Homolka was sent back to Kingston's Prison For Women to resume her sentence. In the summer of 1997, with the closure of the Prison for Women, Homolka was transferred to a minimum-security prison, Joliette Institution, in Joliette, Quebec. Some referred to it as "Club Fed," as a play on the Club Med resorts.

On October 9, 2000, Homolka was moved to a maximum-security psychiatric facility, Saskatoon's Regional Psychiatric Centre in central Saskatchewan, for psychiatric tests which are considered standard procedure in determining one's eligibility for early parole.

In January 2001, Homolka was transferred to Ste-Anne-des-Plaines prison, a maximum-security facility in southwestern Quebec. It was reported that the serial killer had allegedly been the victim of death threats inside prison and on the Internet.

On December 16, 2004, it was determined by the National Parole Board that Homolka had to complete her full prison term, believing her to be a continued risk to perpetrate another crime of violence.

On July 4, 2005, having completed her twelve-year sentence, Karla Homolka was released from Ste-Anne-des-Plaines prison. She moved to Montreal, Quebec, and got married again, having divorced Paul Bernardo in 1994.

In June 2006, it was reported that Homolka sought unsuccessfully to change her name legally to Emily Chiara Tremblay, with Tremblay one of Quebec's most common surnames.

Homolka and her husband had a baby boy and, in 2007, the family moved from Canada to the Antilles in the West Indies in hopes that their one-year-old son could have a "more normal life." Karla Homolka changed her name to Leanne Teale.[20]

On June 16, 2010, with Homolka being eligible to seek a pardon for her conviction on manslaughter charges during that summer, an agreement was "reached between all federal parties to pass a bill that would prevent notorious offenders like Karla Homolka from obtaining a pardon," according to Public Safety Minister Vic Toews.[21]

* * *

Public interest and outrage regarding sex-motivated serial killers Paul Bernardo and Karla Homolka have persisted over the years. This led to production of the controversial movie about the couple, *Karla,* starring Laura Prepon as Homolka and Misha Collins as Bernardo. Told from Homolka's point of view, it was released in Canada in 2006 and a boycott of the film was called for by Ontario Premier Dalton McGuinty.[22]

The deadly sex crimes of Bernardo and Homolka also inspired episodes of several television crime dramas: *The Mentalist*, *Inspector Lynley Mysteries*, *Close to Home*, *Law & Order*, and *CSI: Crime Scene Investigation.*

The serial killer couple has been the subject of cable crime documentaries as well. On the Investigation Discovery series *Wicked Attraction*, its opening episode, "The Perfect Couple," debuted on August 7, 2008; while the series *MSNBC Investigates* examined the tale of Bernardo and Homolka in the episode, "To Love and Kill," shown on May 31, 2002.

* * *

For more riveting stories of serial killer pairs, read the entire book, *Serial Killer Couples: Bonded by Sexual Depravity, Abduction, and Murder*, available in audio, eBook, and print.

# # #

MURDER AND MENACE

Riveting True Crime Tales - Volume 1

(bonus excerpt from the bestselling
true crime anthology)

Missing or Murdered: The Disappearance of Agnes Tufverson

On Monday, December 4, 1933, forty-three-year-old New York corporate attorney Agnes Colonia Tufverson and thirty-three-year-old Ivan Poderjay, a captain in the Yugoslav army, were married in the Little Church Around the Corner in New York City. It seemed like a storybook romance for Agnes, with a bright future of travel and adventure, but it turned out to be anything but that. Two weeks after the couple married, Tufverson mysteriously vanished under suspicious circumstances. She was never to be seen again.

Nearly a century later, the disappearance continues to baffle international law enforcement, true crime buffs, and historians. Was the newlywed bride missing of her own volition? Or was she murdered in what would have been the perfect crime of the century?

* * *

On Tuesday, June 19, 1934, Selma Tufverson sat in the Missing Persons Bureau of the New York Police Department smoking a cigarette as she contemplated what had become a family nightmare. Six months earlier, on Wednesday, December 20, 1933, her older sister Agnes Tufverson had inexplicably gone missing and had yet to resurface. Selma, who lived in Grand Rapids, Michigan, was quite naturally distressed at the notion that Tufverson was most likely dead and the chief suspect in her disappearance was none other than her husband of less than seven months, Captain Ivan Poderjay.

According to Tufverson's sister, she had never met Poderjay in person, but she had spoken to him once on the Tuesday evening of December 19th, when Tufverson phoned to say she and her husband were traveling overseas for their honeymoon. "He really was very charming," Selma admitted in an interview. "He wanted us—my other sisters and me—to come to England sometime."[1] She also confessed that the news that Agnes intended to marry the captain "came as a complete surprise" to her and the entire family.[2]

Born in 1890, Agnes Tufverson had been forced into a maternal role early in life after the death of her mother, in caring for four sisters along with her father, Olaf Tufverson. As a young woman, she was described as "an unusual personality...a vibrant, forceful character—the dominating type [with a] keen mentality."[3] Selma further noted that Tufverson had once been called "Michigan's most intelligent woman, [who] would stand out in any group."[4]

A *McCall's* magazine article on Agnes Tufverson, published in the fall of 1930, was titled "Portia Comes East." It described her as resembling "a blonde heroine of the Siegfried sagas," with her story being one of "a girl who met toil, hardship, and trouble and conquered them all singlehanded[ly]."[5]

While working at a Grand Rapids clothing factory, Tufverson went to school at night. After the war started, she took a job at a real estate office, before relocating to Washington where Tufverson met Ambassador Myron C. Herrick. She later moved to New York to work as his secretary, while taking classes at City College and Columbia University. After gaining her degree, Tufverson started practicing law and went to work for the Electric Bond and Share Company.[6]

According to Selma Tufverson, her sister had not been involved with any men prior to Ivan Poderjay, suggesting that Tufverson had been far too busy between work and school for romance.

Nevertheless, in the spring of 1933, Tufverson found time to take a trip to Europe. It was then that the five-foot-six, slender, attractive attorney presumably first met Ivan Poderjay, who was ten years her junior. Poderjay claimed that they met in July of that year in Britain on a "boat train between London and Southampton."[7]

In any event, when Agnes Tufverson returned to America, she had a new boyfriend with her—Ivan Poderjay. They married a few months later and then lived in Tufverson's apartment at 235 East 22nd Street in New York.

It was three days prior to her wedding day that Tufverson quit her job for what was supposed to be a honeymoon in Europe, followed by a new life in England, where the couple would reside on an estate Poderjay was alleged to own, among several others.

On December 20th, the newlyweds were booked to sail on the S.S. Hamburg for their honeymoon. However, the trip never occurred.

Two days later, Ivan Poderjay boarded the White Star liner Olympic for a trip across the Atlantic. His new wife did not accompany him and had seemed to all but vanish into thin air.

It would later be discovered that on the couple's original day of departure, a cash amount of $25,000 had been withdrawn from Tufverson's bank account. But not a word came from Tufverson as to her whereabouts until Tuesday, January 2, 1934, when she allegedly sent a telegram from London to her sisters, Sally and Olive Tufverson in Grand Rapids, Michigan. It read:

> Bad crossing. Cannot stand fog. Sailing India across France from Marseilles. Eyes better. Happiness to you all through the year.[8]

These were believed to be the last words ever heard from Agnes Tufverson, calling into question whether they actually came from the missing woman who seemingly had everything going for her—making it highly unlikely that she would choose to become a lifelong adventurer, abandoning her family, career, and new husband in the process.

* * *

Ivan Ivanovitch Poderjay was born in Yugoslavia in 1900, moving to Belgrade while he was still young. There he tried his hand at becoming a fortune teller, inventor, and other jobs—none of which stuck. In 1929, Poderjay was alleged to have become engaged to a "socially prominent woman in Copenhagen," before a report surfaced that he was married to someone else in Yugoslavia. Poderjay denied this, but the engagement was called off.[9] Even after leaving Copenhagen, he continued a correspondence relationship with the woman.

In 1930, Poderjay joined the French Foreign Legion and was stationed at Sidi-Bel-Abbes in Algeria, where he reportedly became a Yugoslavian Army Captain.[10]

Months later, Poderjay deserted the Legion and fled to England. There he met and became involved with Marguerite Suzanne Ferrand, a French medical student. On Wednesday, March 22, 1933, Poderjay and Ferrand got married in London.[11]

The two were still married when the handsome Ivan Poderjay wed Agnes Tufverson on December 4th that year.

The bigamy would play a crucial role in Poderjay's life and times, as he became the central figure in the peculiar disappearance of Agnes Tufverson.

* * *

Read the entire riveting historical true crime tale, Missing or Murdered: The Disappearance of Agnes Tufverson and other gripping true stories in *Murder and Menace: Riveting True Crime Tales* (Volumes 1-3) by R. Barri Flowers, available in eBook, audio, and print.

# # #

MURDER CHRONICLES
A Collection of Chilling True Crime Tales
(bonus excerpt from the bestselling true crime anthology)

Murder in Bellevue
The Killing of Alan and Diane Johnson

In the early morning on September 2, 2003, the affluent community of Bellevue, Idaho, was rocked by the murder of residents Alan Scott Johnson and Diane Johnson in their home. Both had been shot to death.[1] Their sixteen-year-old daughter, Sarah Marie Johnson, was in the house when the murder occurred. She ran from the house hysterically shouting that someone had killed her parents.

The tale that emerged was far different, as Sarah Johnson became the chief suspect in her parents' murder in a case of misplaced love, family discord, betrayal, revenge, and violent rage.

As with similar cases of teen familicide (killing of family), parricide (killing of father or mother), patricide (killing of father), and matricide (killing of mother) across the country, this one was no less shocking for its sheer brutality. Few who knew the Johnsons could make sense of the crime or how things could reach such a tragic point within the family.

* * *

By most accounts, in the summer of 2003, Alan Johnson, forty-six, and his wife of twenty years, Diane, fifty-two, had a great life together. They had two children: Matt, twenty-two (Diane's son from a previous relationship), and Sarah Marie, sixteen. The Johnsons had a nice home in Bellevue, Idaho, in Blaine County's Wood River Valley, just south of the resort city of Sun Valley. Alan co-owned a landscaping business and Diane was employed by a medical clinic.

But their storybook life ended tragically when Alan and Diane Johnson were shot to death in their home just after Labor Day on September 2, 2003. Diane was shot in the head while she lay sleeping in bed. Then Alan was shot in the chest above his heart, his body still wet after just leaving the shower.

As police arrived and took in the ghastly site of two adults dead from gunshots, the crime scene was quickly secured for possible evidence and to perhaps catch a killer.

According to Blaine County Sheriff Walt Femling, the crime scene was the worst he could remember ever seeing, noting, "There was blood and hair on the carpet. It was on the ceiling. It was on all the walls. There was part of a skull cap in the hallway."[2]

Investigators "found a trail of blood spatters, tissue, and bone fragments that went from the Johnson's bedroom into the hall, and across to [their daughter] Sarah Johnson's bedroom," which was about twenty feet away.[3]

The police went into full investigation mode, blocking off the street and searching a garbage truck that had just picked up trash from the house. In it was a treasure trove of DNA evidence on "a bloody bathrobe, a left-handed leather glove, and a right-handed latex glove."[4]

More evidence was found inside, including in the master bedroom where a .264 Winchester Magnum rifle, along with two butcher knives were situated at the bottom of the victim's bed. In Sarah's room, authorities also discovered an ammunition magazine.

An important item that detectives noted was the lack of any sign of forced entry in the Johnson's home, suggesting that the killer either had a key or was let in.

They turned their attention to Alan and Diane Johnson's sixteen-year-old daughter, Sarah.

* * *

Read the entire riveting historical true crime tale, Murder in Bellevue: The Killing of Alan and Diane Johnson, and other gripping stories in the bestselling anthology, *Murder Chronicles: A Collection of Chilling True Crime Tales* by R. Barri Flowers, available in audio, eBook, and print.

\# \# \#

NOTES

Killer of Her Husband's Secretary

1. "Slaying Rival Laid to Jealousy," *Los Angeles Times* (August 15, 1935), p. 3.

2. Eileen Morey, *Amelia Earhart* (San Diego, CA: Lucent Books, 1995); Doris L. Rich, *Amelia Earhart: A Biography* (Washington, DC: Smithsonian Institution Press, 1989).

3. "Babe Ruth Biography," Biography, https://www.biography.com/people/babe-ruth-9468009.

4. Wikipedia, the Free Encyclopedia, "1935 in the United States," https://en.wikipedia.org/wiki/1935_in_the_United_States.

5. R. Barri Flowers and H. Loraine Flowers, *Murders in the United States: Crimes, Killers and Victims of the Twentieth Century* (Jefferson, NC:

McFarland, 2004), pp. 47-48; "Bruno Hauptmann: German-American Convict," Encyclopedia Britannica, https://www.britannica.com/biography/Bruno-Hauptmann.

6. "Ma Barker Biography," Biography, https://www.biography.com/people/ma-barker-14515515; Robert Winter, *Mean Men: The Sons of Ma Barker* (Danbury, CT: Routledge, 2000).

7. William Ivy Hair, *The Kingfish and His Realm: The Life and Times of Huey P. Long* (Baton Rouge, LA: Louisiana State University Press, 1996); "Huey Long," History, https://www.history.com/topics/huey-long.

8. Marda Liggett Woodbury, *Stopping the Presses: The Murder of Walter W. Liggett* (Minneapolis: University of Minnesota Press, 1998).

9. From Wikipedia, the Free Encyclopedia, "Queens," https://en.wikipedia.org/wiki/Queens.

10. Ibid.

11. David Hartman and Barry Lewis, "A Walk Through Queens," Thirteen Media With Impact, https://www.thirteen.org/queens/history3.html.

12. James Mauro, *Twilight At The World of Tomorrow: Genius, Madness, Murder, and the 1939 World's Fair on the Brink of War* (New York: Ballantine, 2010).

13. From Wikipedia, the Free Encyclopedia, "Beechhurst, Queens," https://en.wikipedia.org/wiki/Beechhurst,_Queens.

14. Quoted in "Wife's Bullets Write Finis to Triangle," *Akron Beacon Journal* (August 15, 1935), p. 8; "Wife Confesses She Killed Rival," *New York Times* (August 15, 1935).

15. Quoted in "Wife 'Killer of the Other Woman'," *Star Tribune* (August 16, 1935), p. 6.

16. "Slayer to Plead Insanity," *New York Times* (August 16, 1935).

17. "Wife's Bullets Write Finis to Triangle;" "Domestic Triangle Ends in Violent Tragedy," *Akron Beacon Journal* (August 15, 1935), p. 1.

18. Quoted in "Slayer of Love Rival Told Police of Gun an Hour Before Tragedy," *Brooklyn Daily Eagle* (September 7, 1935), p. 22; Dorothy Roe, "Slayer of Former Braddock Girl Sobs in Court," *Pittsburgh Post-Gazette* (December 18, 1935), p. 5.

19. "Wife Confesses She Killed Rival."

20. Ibid.

21. Quoted in "Wife's Bullets Write Finis to Triangle."

22. "Slain Girl's Friends, Kin Recall School Days Here," *Pittsburgh Post-Gazette* (August 16, 1935), p. 2.

23. Quoted in Dorothy Rue, "State to Ask Death For Killer of Former Braddock Girl," *Pittsburgh Post-Gazette* (August 16, 1935), p. 2.

24. "Queens Prosecutor to Seek First-Degree Murder Charge," *New York Times* (August 20, 1935).

25. Ibid.; "Grand Jury Gets Case of Wife Charged With Killing Secretary," *New York Times* (September 7, 1935).

26. "Slayer of Love Rival Told Police of Gun."

27. Ibid.

28. Ibid.

29. Ibid.

30. "Mrs. Reisman Indicted," *New York Times* (September 20, 1935), p. 24.

31. "Reisman Trial Oct. 14," *New York Times* (September 24, 1935).

32. "Reisman Defense Stresses 'Mishap'," *New York Times* (December 18, 1935), p. 35.

33. Ibid.

34. Ibid.

35. Ibid.

36. Ibid.

37. Roc, "Slayer of Former Braddock Girl Sobs in Court."

38. "Mrs. Reisman Sobs on Telling Story," *New York Times* (December 19, 1935), p. 28.

39. Ibid.

40. Roe, "Slayer of Former Braddock Girl Sobs in Court."

41. "Mrs. Reisman Sobs on Telling Story."

42. Quoted in ibid.

43. Ibid.

44. Ibid.

45. Ibid.

46. "Slayer of Husband's Sweetheart Guilty of Manslaughter," *Kane Republican* (December 20, 1935), p. 1.

47. Ibid.

48. Ibid.

49. "Women Aid Mrs. Reisman," *New York Times* (December 22, 1935), p. 13.

50. Quoted in "Plead for Mrs. Reisman," *New York Times* (December 23, 1935).

51. "Escapes Prison in Killing Girl," *Reading Times* (December 24, 1935), p. 4.

52. "Woman Freed in Killing of Rival in Love," *Pittsburgh Post-Gazette* (December 24, 1935), p. 2.

53. "Escapes Prison in Killing Girl."

54. "Mrs. Reisman is Free; Term is Suspended," *New York Times* (December 24, 1935), p. 1.

55. Quoted in ibid. *See also* "Woman Convicted in Killing of Husband's Secretary," *St. Louis Post-Dispatch* (December 21, 1935), p. 3.

56. "Mrs. Reisman is Free; Term is Suspended."

57. Quoted in "Colden Defends Reisman Release," *New York Times* (December 25, 1935).

58. "Mrs. Reisman is Free; Term is Suspended."

59. Ibid.

60. Quoted in ibid.

61. "Seigh Pursues Mrs. Reisman in Girl Killing," *Brooklyn Daily Eagle* (March 14, 1936), p. 2.

62. Quoted in ibid.

63. "Reisman Writ is Denied," *New York Times* (October 28, 1938), p. 1.

64. Ibid.

Serial Killer Couples: Paul Bernardo and Karla Homolka

1. Wikipedia, the Free Encyclopedia, "Paul Bernardo," http://en.wikipedia.org/wiki/Paul_Bernardo#cite_note-Pron2005-2.

2. Ibid. *See also* R. Barri Flowers and H. Loraine Flowers, *Murders in the United States:*

Crimes, Killers and Victims of the Twentieth Century (Jefferson, NC: McFarland, 2004), pp. 3-5.

3. "Paul Bernardo."

4. Ibid.

5. Wikipedia, the Free Encyclopedia, "Karla Homolka," http://en.wikipedia.org/wiki/Karla_Homolka#cite_note-4. *See also* Stephen Williams, *Invisible Darkness: The Strange Case Of Paul Bernardo and Karla Homolka* (New York: Bantam, 1997).

6. "Paul Bernardo."

7. Ibid.

8. Ibid.; Williams, *Invisible Darkness.*

9. Marilyn Bardsley, "Paul Bernardo & Karla Homolka," TruTv Crime Library, http://www.trutv.com/library/crime/serial_killers/notorious/bernardo/murder_3.html.

10. "Paul Bernardo."

11. "Karla Homolka."

12. Bardsley, "Paul Bernardo & Karla Homolka."

13. Ibid.

14. "Karla Homolka."

15. Ibid.

16. Ibid.

17. Wikipedia, the Free Encyclopedia, "Dangerous Offender," http://en.wikipedia.org/wiki/Dangerous_Offender.

18. Marilyn Bardsley, "Paul Bernardo & Karla Homolka."

19. "Key Events in the Bernardo/Homolka Case," *CBC News Canada* (June 17, 2010), http://www.cbc.ca/news/canada/story/2010/06/16/f-bernardo-homolka-timeline.html.

20. "Karla Homolka."

21. "Key Events in the Bernardo/Homolka Case."

22. "Karla Homolka."

Murder and Menace: Missing or Murdered

1. "Sister of Miss Tufverson Says Here That Poderjay Captivated Even Her," *New York Times* (June 20, 1934).

2. Ibid.

3. Ibid.

4. Ibid.

5. Quoted in *McCall's* (Fall 1930).

6. Doris Lane, "The Case of the Vanishing Bride," Author's Den (February 12, 2003), http://www.authorsden.com/visit/viewarticle.asp?id=1917.

7. "Poderjay Receives 2 1/2 to 5 Year Term," *New York Times* (March 22, 1935);"The Scene of the Perfect Crime--No. 235 E. 22nd St.," Daytonian in Manhattan (April 10, 2013), http://daytoninmanhattan.blogspot.com/2013/04/the-scene-of-perfect-crime-no-235-e.html.

8. Quoted in Mark Chirnside and Jack Wetton, "The Poderjay Case," www.markchirnside.co.uk.

9. "Engaged in Copenhagen: Poderjay was to Have Wed Society Leader There in 1929," *New York Times* (June 30, 1934).

10. Ibid.

11. "Poderjay Quits Cell to get Clothing," *New York Times* (August 13, 1934).

Murder Chronicles: Murder in Bellevue

1. R. Barri Flowers, *The Dynamics of Murder: Kill or Be Killed* (Boca Raton, FL: CRC Press, 2012), pp. 273-76.

2. Elizabeth R. Grodd and Jeffrey L. Diamond, "Primetime Crime: Teen Charged With Parents' Gruesome Murder," *ABC Primetime* (August 13, 2008), http://abcnews.go.com/TheLaw/story?id=3451371&page=1.

3. Charles Montaldo, "Profile of Idaho Teen Killer Sarah Johnson," *About News*, http://crime.about.com/od/juvenile/a/sarah_johnson.htm.

4. Grodd and Diamond, "Primetime Crime."

# # #

ABOUT THE AUTHOR

R. Barri Flowers is a well-respected criminologist and bestselling author of more than one hundred books, including enthralling true crime and criminology books, as well as gripping mystery, suspense, and thriller fiction, and young adult mysteries.

True crime titles include The Sex Slave Murders, Masters of True Crime (editor), Murder and Menace: Riveting True Crime Tales (volumes 1-3); Murder Chronicles: A Collection of Chilling True Crime Tales; Murders in the United States; Serial Killer Couples: Bonded by Sexual Depravity, Abduction and Murder; and The Dreadful Acts of Jack the Ripper and Other True Tales of Serial Murder and Prostitutes.

Mystery and thriller fiction titles include Before He Kills Again, Dark Streets of Whitechapel, Dead in Pukalani, Killer in The Woods, Murder in Maui, Murder in Honolulu, Murdered in the Man Cave, Murdered in the Gourmet Kitchen, Murder of the Hula Dancers, Murder on Kaanapali Beach,

Persuasive Evidence, Seduced to Kill in Kauai, State's Evidence, and Justice Served.

As an expert on violent criminality, R. Barri Flowers has appeared on the Biography Channel, Investigation Discovery, and Oxygen television documentary crime series.

Follow R. Barri Flowers on Twitter, Facebook, LinkedIn, Pinterest, YouTube, Flickr, Goodreads, and LibraryThing. Learn more about the author in Wikipedia and www.rbarriflowers.com.

# # #

Printed in Great Britain
by Amazon

39466871R00050